carolinda tolstoy **ceramics**

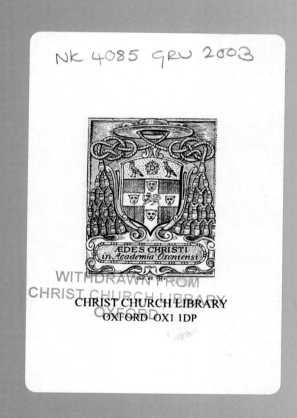
ernst j. grube

carolinda tolstoy **ceramics**

ernst j. grube

Art Books International

contents

Countess Carolinda Tolstoy's pottery occupies a very special position within the art of contemporary ceramic-making. Descendant of an old Middle Eastern family, linked to one of the great families of Russia, and living in London, her art draws on a variety of sources. Some of her shapes are those of conventional bottles and bowls but others follow shapes used by Muslim potters; some, at her own suggestion, are inspired by the famous and curious onion-shaped domes of Russian churches [No. 1; see also Nos. 3 & 4]. But as is evident from even a superficial acquaintance with her work, her principal inspiration is the pottery of the Muslim Middle East. Sidestepping the Far Eastern mode in which so many English potters of the 20th century have worked — notably Bernard Leach and his school, she appears to have taken up, in a

unique way, the tradition of the perpetuation of Near Eastern pottery design by European artists.

Fascinated by both the floral and the abstract geometric patterns of Islamic art, she has developed a style of ceramic painting that combines elements of both these forms of decoration, mixing various elements in a highly imaginative way: while principally using one specific form of flower in a pattern [Nos. 14 to 29], she often combines different flowers in one design [Nos. 30 to 34], creating patterns of great beauty and energy. Indeed, in the majority of her patterns she takes off on the traditions of ceramic decoration that go back to the 16th-century Ottoman Turkish ateliers which flourished in many parts of the Ottoman realm. Especially the designs on architectural tile work had a profound impact on ceramic design for many centuries in almost all parts of the Muslim world; it received equal recognition, and enjoyed an almost uninterrupted success, all over Europe.

The most impressive reflection of Ottoman floral ceramic

fig 1

fig 2

fig 3

fig 4

decoration, which reached its peak in the ateliers of Iznik and Kütahya, can be found in Italy. Italian ceramicists developed their polychrome painted maiolicas into one of the greatest manifestations of ceramics as an art form. They were deeply impressed by Islamic patterns and followed them in many variations throughout the 16th and 17th centuries. Realistic floral patterns appear to have had the greatest attraction for artists and collectors. In their infinitely varied combinations of tulips and carnations, interspersed with equally elaborate and naturalistic representations of other flowers — roses, hyacinths and frittilaries — Turkish pottery displays floral patterns of unparalleled vitality and great beauty. Its intense polychromy, dominated by red and blue blossoms and deep green leaves and stalks, at times enhanced by the addition of overglaze applications of gold [fig 1], was adopted by Italian artists from the 17th century onwards. The atelier that immediately comes to mind is that of Candia, near Padova, from which dated pieces are recorded from the early 17th century [fig 2]. This early impact of Ottoman designs on those of Italian ceramic artists stands at the beginning of a tradition into which Carolinda Tolstoy's pottery fits in most immediately.

But it is not only the Italian Candiana wares that represent this European fascination with Islamic pottery decoration; many parallel movements also give evidence of Ottoman floral patterns as a principal source of ceramic decoration. In Italy, the tradition lasts well into the 19th and even the beginning of the 20th century in the Cantagalli studios of Florence [fig 3]. But there is striking evidence for the success of Ottoman ceramic painters elsewhere in the West,

principally in the creations of the Zsolnay Manufactory of Pecs in Hungary [fig 4]. Here, forms of the purest Ottoman design were fashioned, often in close collaboration with artists from many other parts of Europe, notably France. Theodore Deck, who had established himself in Paris towards the middle of the 19th century and who recreated a variety of Islamic art forms — including metalwork — in the medium of glazed ceramic, designed Ottoman floral patterns for Zsolnay. He was perhaps the most influential European artist to make use of Oriental ceramic decoration, especially in the Ottoman polychrome floral style. But British potters, among them most notably William De Morgan, occupy an equally significant position. De Morgan, probably the greatest of the

fig 6

fig 7

fig 8

"Orientalist" potters, not only embraced the full range of Ottoman floral design [fig 5] but he also developed many of these forms further, creating a truly original style of ceramic decoration [fig 6]. And while his floral patterns are particularly elaborate and influential, he was also among the first to make full use of the art of lustre-painting [fig 7]. Decorating a surface by painting it with metallic lustre, which forms a significant part of Carolinda Tolstoy's designs, was a technique invented by Muslim potters of the Abbasid period in the early 9th century; it continued to be produced throughout the history of Muslim ceramic making. The technique had been adopted in the West by the ceramic ateliers in Spain; Spanish lustre ware was then exported to all parts of Europe and the rest of the world. From its very beginning, it enjoyed particular favour with collectors after the transfer of the factories from Andalucia to Valencia, following the reconquest of Northern Spain by the Christians. The great armorial plates, and many other typical shapes as well [fig 8], were almost immediately imitated in the West, especially in Italy and France, and after a certain decline of the Spanish production in the 17th and 18th centuries, a conscious attempt was made in the 19th century to recreate the 15th-century style.

The origin of lustre-painted pottery in Italy is not entirely clear, but there can be little question that Hispano-Moresque ware was a major inspiration. Although there is still some uncertainty as to where lustre-painting was first practiced in Italy, today it seems generally accepted that the workshops of Deruta, a small town in Umbria, near Perugia, first used

metallic lustre-painting to decorate Italian maiolica [fig 9]. It was soon practiced in several other towns, but the brilliance of the silver and gold Deruta lustre was never matched by the other factories. Deruta and Gubbio (the second important centre of lustre-painting on maiolica) attracted artists from many different places in Italy to work for local potters, but they appear never to have stayed long nor did they ever become part of the local workshops. In contrast to the wares from other factories, Deruta pieces often display non-figurative designs of abstract floral patterns, which closely resemble the arabesque designs ultimately derived from the Muslim world. A variety of abstract patterns covering the entire surface of a

fig 9

fig 10

fig 11

plate or bowl were popular in Deruta and may have been derived from the same source. Gubbio, which produced a deep red, rather than a silvery golden lustre [fig 10], is equally original in its approach to surface decoration and its abstract tendency appears to have been as strong as, if not actually stronger, than that of Deruta.

Despite the splendour of lustre decorated maiolica, it does not seem to have enjoyed popularity for a long time and it would seem that, after a very early date in the 16th century, only single pieces, rather than series of them, were produced, which must have been made for special occasions or specific purposes. Gubbio, specializing in a variety of smaller objects of more practical use, continued to make lustre-wares of fine quality, until at least the later 16th century, but the quality of Deruta lustre deteriorated towards the end of the 16th century; only quite poor wares, clearly for a market other than the nobility, were made in the later 17th century. The technique, as a manner of decorating ceramic wares, then seems to have been discarded and forgotten.

Lustre was rediscovered at the beginning of the 19th century but, curiously, attracted little interest at first, ceramic factories of the time not finding any real commercial potential in wares requiring such complex and unstable conditions of production. A true revival began by the middle of the 19th century and gathered momentum towards the end of the century and it continues to be popular to this day. The revival — or better perhaps, the re-discovery — of lustre decoration in pottery is closely linked to the experimentation, by European potteries, with the gilding of ceramic surfaces. Immensely desirable and always, in the production of

porcelain in Europe, an essential decorative element, the touches of gold (for real gold leaf, or powdered gold, was used) that enhanced the aesthetic and social appeal of ceramic table ware in the 18th century became both a technical and a financial burden. Gilding was expensive; as it wore off rather quickly, sounder technical and economically more efficient methods had to be found.

It was in England that a technical breakthrough came about. John Hancock of the Spode factory re-discovered the method of lustering a ceramic surface, a discovery that was immediately adopted by none other than Josiah Wedgwood and, soon, by others as well. Although Wedgwood had taken out a patent on the "ornamenting Earthen and Porcelain ware with an encaustic Gold Bronze" (revived again in the 20th century [fig 11]), he did not enforce it; thus, in the mid-18th century England, lustre was more generally utilized, once again, in the decoration of pottery. At first lustre was not used as true painting — just as at the very beginning of the process in 9th-century Muslim Iraq — but as a thin metallic film, applied over a clear glaze to give the object the appearance of being made of silver or gold. Technical difficulties, rather than deliberate choice, led to the use of differently-coloured lustre decoration in the Staffordshire factories. Not before the revival of lustre-painting in Italy and the re-discovery, in the mid-19th century, of the 15th-century ruby-red lustre, by Pietro Gai (director of a ceramic factory in Pesaro), was ruby-red lustre again fully developed. Gai came to England in 1862, visiting the Wedgwood, Minton and Copeland factories and hoping to be hired as a designer, in which he was unsuccessful. But he did sell his ruby-lustre

fig 12

fig 13

fig 14

recipe to the Wedgwood factory. Still, the technological problems were not entirely resolved and it was only after further experimentation, both by the Wedgwoods and by the French ceramic painter Emile Lessore, who had been put in charge of art pottery in the Wedgwood factory in 1865, that ruby-red and gold-orange lustre were successfully produced. Other factories, especially Minton, William De Morgan [fig 7], Maw and Co. of Jackfield, Pilkington's Royal Lancastrian Pottery in Manchester [fig 12] and the Ruskin Pottery of Edward Richard and William Howson Taylor, all produced lustre in the later 19th and the beginning of the 20th century, the Royal Lancastrian Pottery remaining active until 1937.

The best known among the many artists and factories that began to work again in this medium in this period is undoubtedly William De Morgan who actually claimed to have rediscovered, around 1870, the "lost art of Moorish or Gubbio lustres", though acknowledging the fact that in Italy lustre had already been used somewhat earlier. His deep red lustre-painted wares and tiles are without parallel even in the earliest red-lustre wares of the Abbasid period; his designs, ranging from the truly neo-Oriental (mostly in his polychrome pieces) to the extraordinarily evocative and fantastic, captured the imagination of his contemporaries [fig 13]. The impact of De Morgan's work on both later art potters and eventually on industrial ceramic production in England was immense, the lustre pottery and tiles of the Maw factory being a particularly good example [fig 14]. Yet it seems that this remarkable revival of an ancient form of ceramic decoration gradually faded from favour and it was only in quite recent years that a second revival took place. This

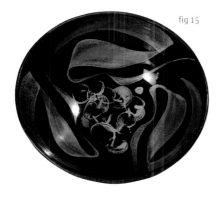

fig 15

fig 16

fig 17

second revival was mainly brought about by a group of English art potters who concentrated on the use of lustre, prime among them being Alan Caiger-Smith who took his cue from the earliest forms of the technique in the Islamic world. In fact he uses almost exclusively monochrome deep red, or brownish-red, lustre as the main medium of decoration. With some pieces, his models quite obviously lie in the works of the Abbasid ateliers, but most of his oeuvre is a completely original creation [fig 15]. It could best be described as paying unparalleled homage to the genius of Islamic ceramic artists but it may equally be said that, as works of ceramic art, his wares stand entirely on their own. Sutton Taylor has gone a step further in the use of lustre, very likely inspired by the styles of polychrome lustre-painting in the early Muslim ateliers [fig 16]. But he rarely adopts patterns or designs used by Muslim potters, his wares showing instead an almost entirely abstract play of variations on the ancient theme of polychrome surface decoration [fig 17], although at times floral elements appear that have a distinctly Oriental flavour [fig 18].

fig 18

fig 19

fig 20

fig 22

fig 21

fig 23

fig 24

Carolinda Tolstoy uses lustre in still a different way. The pinkish colour of her lustre accords in with her very personal colour scheme, but it is a colour that had been popular for a certain period with English potters, in the 18th and early 19th century [fig 19] and it owes little to Islamic models. In fact, in almost all ways her "borrowing" of design motifs from Islamic models is most clearly paralleled not by Caiger-Smith and Sutton Taylor, the master potters of contemporary England, but by early 20th century movements in Holland and France. At the turn of the 20th century, the world-famous Delft factories developed a style of ceramic decoration that lasted into the 1950's: it embraces a large variety of Islamic shapes and decorative designs, from mediaeval Seljuq lustre-wares [figs 20 & 21] to 16th-and 17th-century Safavid and Ottoman polychrome floral patterns [fig 22]. Many of them find close parallels in Carolinda Tolstoy's pottery. Even more striking, because of the choice of colours, are the works of French ceramic artists of the Fauve movement. The closest in spirit is the work of André Matthey [figs 23 & 24] but even certain ceramics decorated by André Derain, Henri Matisse [fig 25] and Maurice de Vlaminck [fig. 26] show the continuous fascination of contemporary artists with the shapes, the colours, and even the individual forms of Islamic ceramic designs.

fig 25

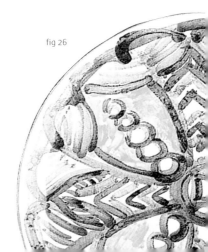

fig 26

2000 | 19 × 24cm

beginnings

2002 | 38×18cm

Turning, now, to Carolinda Tolstoy's ceramics, one is struck by her pieces which are, as is perhaps to be expected, very close to the models of her inspiration — Ottoman pottery. Both the scale-patterned vase [No. 8], an almost direct take-off of an identical Ottoman type, and the octagonal tile which shows tulips and roses arranged around a central medallion [No. 10], using the rock-and-wave pattern so frequently found on Iznik plates as a border design, are good examples of this early stage of the artist's approach to her sources. But most other early pieces are only loosely based on such models, using scrolls with attached abstract floral elements or flowering shrubs arranged around the shape of the object in a fashion that recall the realistic floral patterns of Iznik pottery but are rather different in her choice of blossoms and colour. Some combine various elements of these models in a manner that removes the patterns from the immediate sources, both in shapes and colours. Tulip-shapes, for instance, are often ambiguous and could be mistaken for slender pomegranates [No. 2]; on the other hand true pomegranate patterns also appear [No. 9], a form that does not find true parallels in Ottoman designs. Finally, tentative arabesque scrolls make their first appearance [Nos. 12 & 13], a form that will be developed further in later pieces.

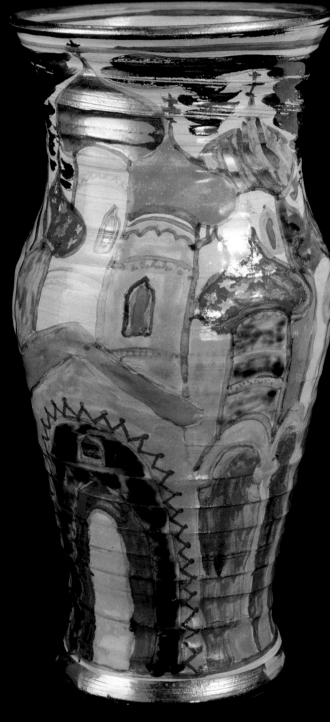

2000 | 25 × 17

2003 | 36 × 21 cm

beginnings

2003 | 38 × 29

2003   39 × 26 cm

1999 | 35 × 35 cm

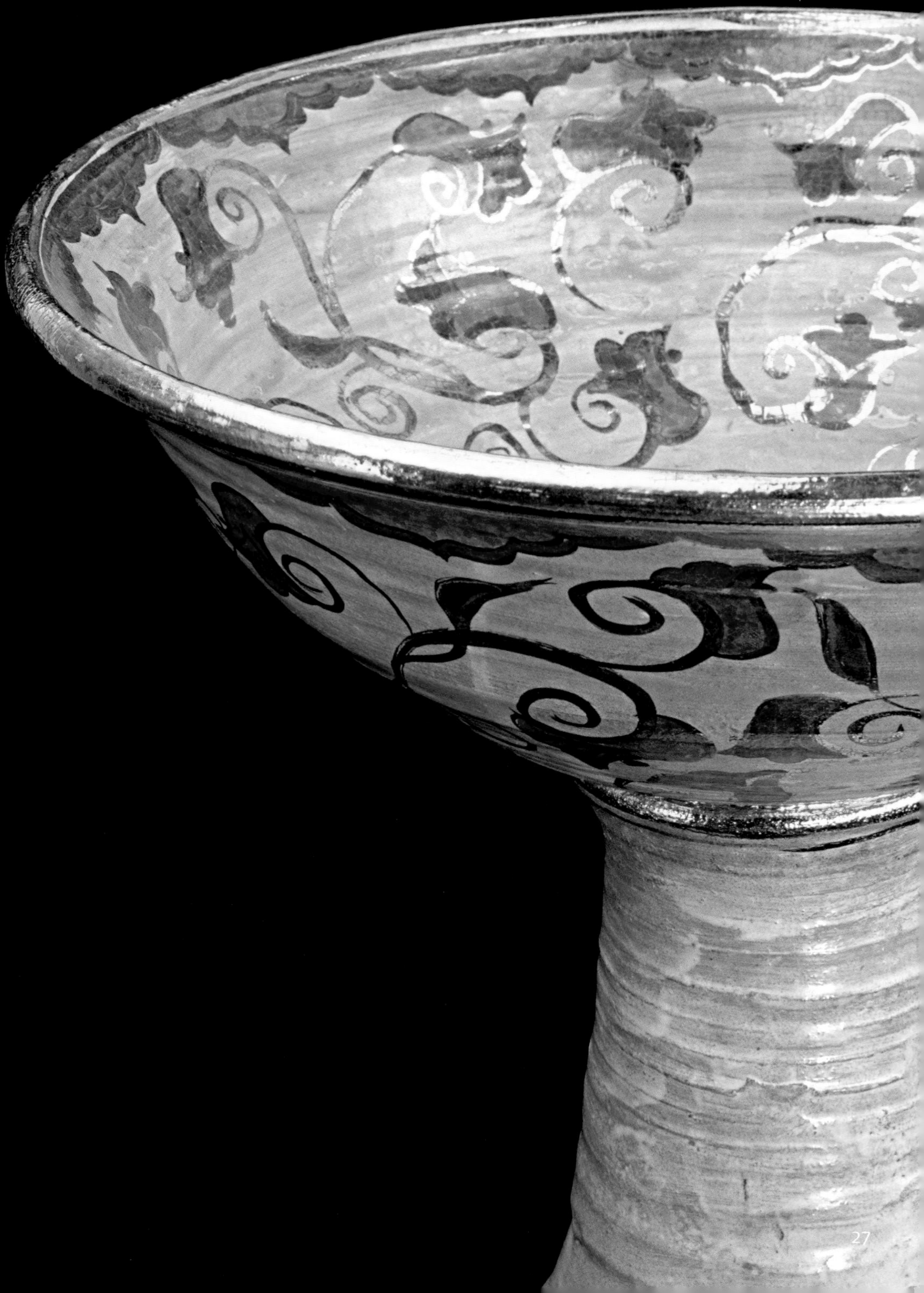

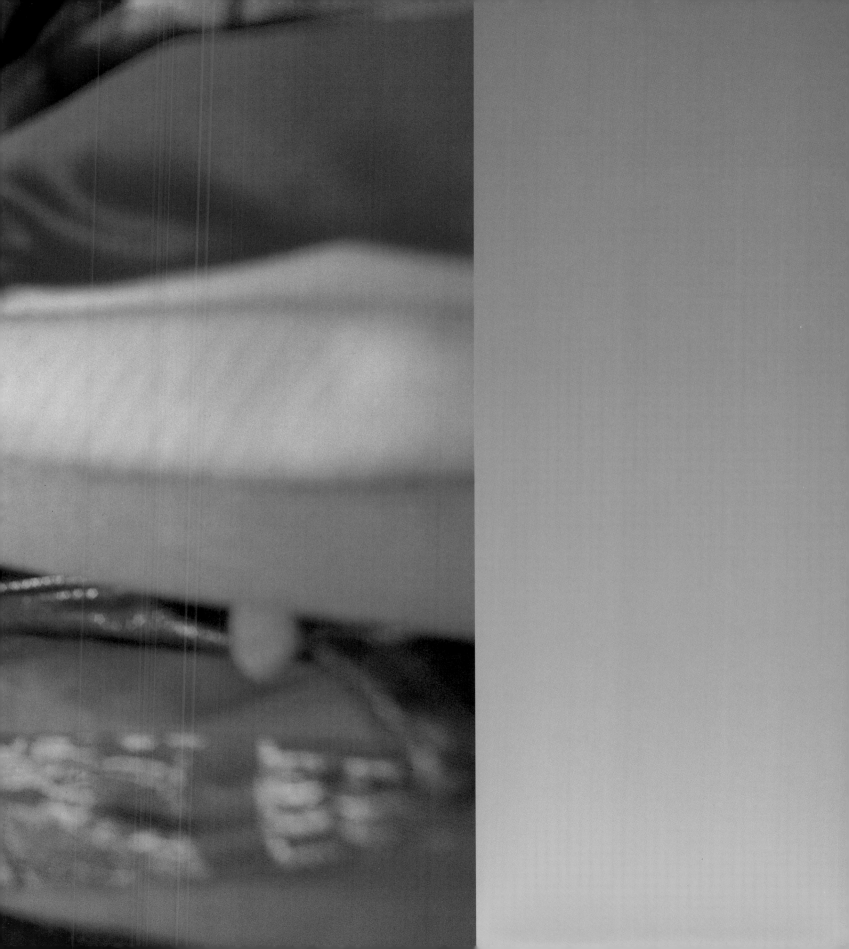

2003 | 35 × 18 cm

t u l i p s

The Tulip, the Turkish flower plays a major role in Carolinda Tolstoy's ceramic patterns. But while her first renderings of the flower are quite realistic, both in shape and colour [Nos. 14 to 18], very soon they take on a life of their own; the tulips are executed in black with a gold outline [No. 19], or are altogether gold on a black ground [No. 20].

t u l i p s

tulips

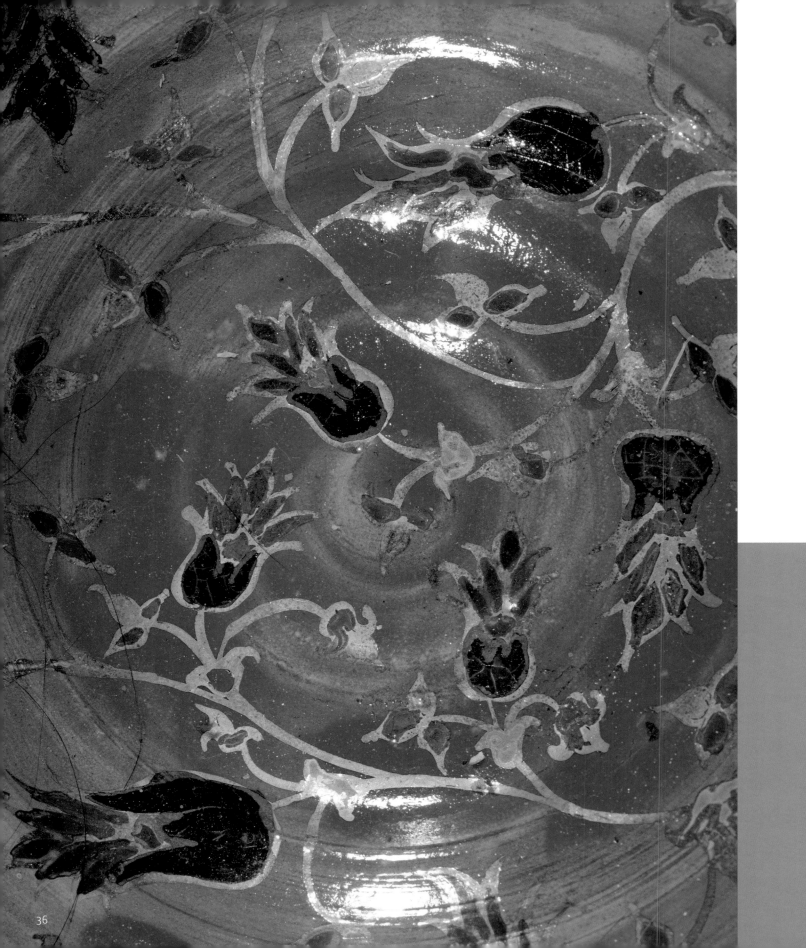

t u l i p s

Exactly where the left side of the
colonnade now begins, was the start
of the Circus initiated by Caligula and
completed by Nero almost two thousand years ago. It was very long so
that there could be chariot races, and
it ended well beyond the point where
the apse of the To its right was the Via
Cornelia and, immediately beyond, a
vast cemetery. There, as we know,
Saint Peter was buried.As an embellishment for the Circus, in 37 ad
Caligula ordered that a huge obelisk
decoratTo its right was the Via
Cornelia and, immediately beyond, a
vast cemetery. There, as we know,
Saint Peter was buried.

tulips

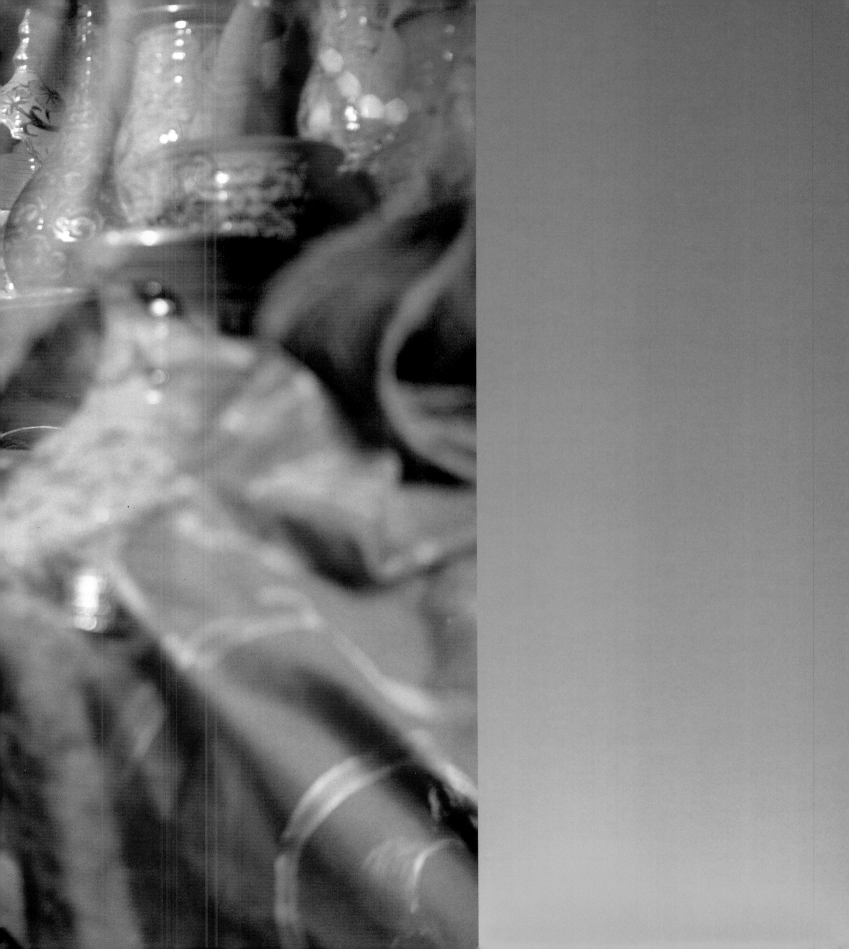

c a r n a t i o n s

An equally significant transformation of the true appearance of the flower takes place in her use of the carnation, the second most frequently encountered blossom in Ottoman design. While at first she uses a daring combination of the natural red of the blossom with an unusual blue [No. 21], or the natural red of the blossom becomes a mere outline encasing the gold rays of the inner petals [Nos. 22 & 23], eventually the carnation blossoms exchange their natural red for a variety of blue hues [Nos. 25 to 29], an interpretation carried on into the next pattern group.

1982 | 10 × 27 cm

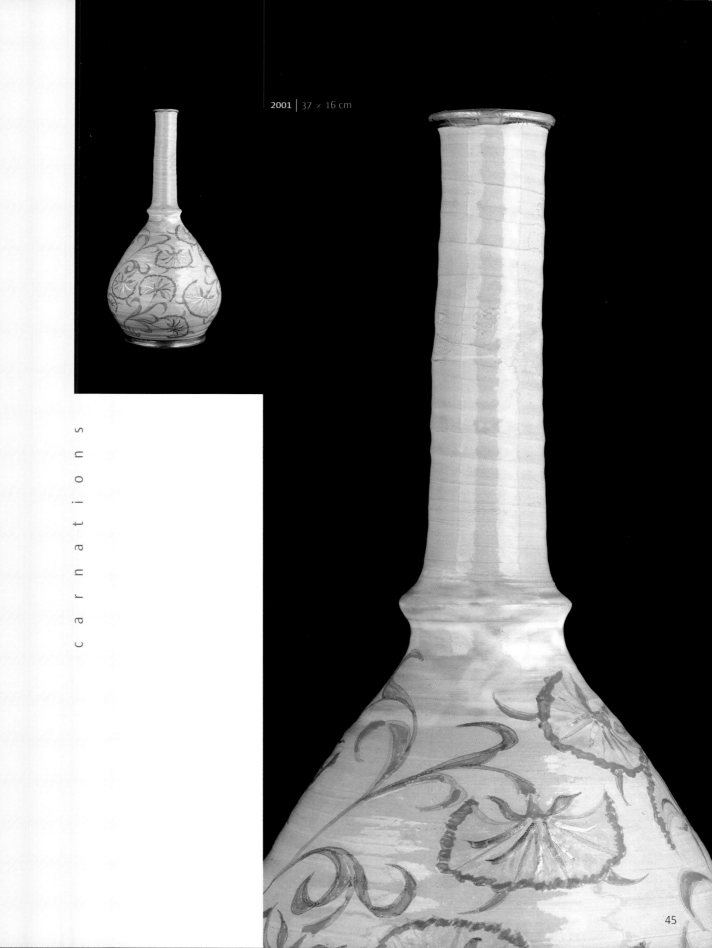

2001 | 37 × 16 cm

carnations

45

1999 | 9 × 23 cm

carnations

2001 | 15 × 38 cm

carnations

carnations

carnations

2001 | 16 × 38 cm

Here the blue carnation is combined with the red tulip, but both blossoms are richly endowed with gold, both for the inner articulation of the carnation petals and the enhancement of the tulip blossom [30 to 34], a technique which was equally-if rarely — used by Ottoman potters.

2001   11 × 23 cm

2001 | 16 × 38 cm

2002 | 4 × 21 cm   2002 | 6 × 30 cm

s e p a r a t i o n

While the majority of her purely floral designs maintain an essentially naturalistic rendering of flowers attached to undulating floral stems that, at times, develop into scrolls, the fascination of the abstract, geometric element of Muslim design eventually takes over. In this group of patterns, the natural flower shrubs are encased in leaf-shaped medallions or cartouches — four of them dividing the circular shape of the decorated plate [Nos. 35 to 37]. Blue carnations, black tulips, and altogether golden stems and blossoms fill these units, the spaces in between the cartouches being filled with golden scroll work, gold being used also for minor details-leaves, stems, and eventually for the entire floral and geometric patterns. The distance between the model and the final design has grown ever greater.

separation

2002 | 5 × 26 cm

Gold is the primary colour for yet another floral pattern group. Here open or closed lily blossoms — curiously sickle-shaped in the first [No. 39], and trumpet-shaped in the second [Nos. 40 & 41] — are attached to free-flowing scrolls or to more traditionally arranged floral shrubs. While the first form is executed entirely in gold, most of the detail of the second group is equally drawn in gold, the pale blue blossoms being the only element painted in blue. Yet another piece develops the lily blossom in a manner that creates a renewed ambiguity: the distinction between one floral form and another is almost obliterated and a new hybrid — the lily-carnation — emerges [No. 42].

lillies

2003 | 25 × 28 cm

l i l l i e s

Exactly where the left side of the colonnade now begins, was the start of the Circus initiated by Caligula and completed by Nero almost two thousand years ago. It was very long so that there could be chariot races, and it ended well beyond the point where the apse of the present basilica now stands.

To its right was the Via Cornelia and, immediately beyond, a vast cemetery. There, as we know, Saint Peter was buried.

As an embellishment for the Circus, in 37 ad Caligula ordered that a huge obelisk decorating the Forum of Julius Caesar in Alexandria be brought from Egypt to Rome.

Around 67 ad, Saint Peter and nine hundred other Christian martyrs were put to death in the Circus. The obelisk, which at one time was located in the middle of the long Circus, witnessed the sufferings of the martyrs and, in particular, the death of the apostle Peter, who, according to ancient tradition, was crucified iuxta obeliscum, beside the obelisk.

2003 25 × 28 cm

2002 43 × 22 cm

lillies

2000 | 37 × 16 cm

Scroll-work, in its infinite variety of articulations, is unquestionably one of the fundamental elements of pattern and design in the Muslim world. Its potential for filling almost any given space or covering any given form or shape makes it the ideal medium for an almost unlimited number of applications, from the simple leafy stem scroll to the infinite pattern of the arabesque. Scroll work is used in just such a manner in Carolinda Tolstoy's ceramic decorations. It appears in the simple inward curling variety with short, single-leaf attachments [Nos. 43 to 50], or enclosing in the curving circular movements small buds or blossom-shaped units [Nos. 51 to 54]. Most of these scrolls, all executed in gold, are displayed in loose arrangements that leave free of patterns a great deal of the strong-coloured background.

scrolls | iskander

1998 | 35 × 25 cm

84

2000 | 18 × 12 cm

scrolls | iskander

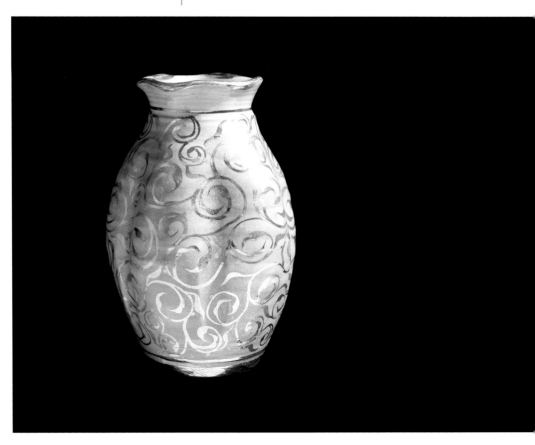

scrolls | iskander

scrolls | iskander

2000 | 17 × 11 cm

scrolls | iskander

2003 | 16 × 10 cm

scrolls | iskander

2002 | 11 × 29 cm

A second variation on the theme of the leafy scroll consists of elegant free-floating lancette-leaf branches interconnected by thin, often quite long stems from which spring leaves that, at times, take on a life of their own. Some of them extend beyond the ordinary leaf-shape, suggesting birds or snakes in their undulating extensions rather than vegetal elements [Nos. 57 & 58]. This ambiguity of distinction between floral and zoomorphic forms is, of course, an ancient and typical conceit in Islamic design: it is only very tentatively hinted at in some of these patterns, but it is equally difficult to ignore. At the same time, one is strongly reminded of certain floral decorations on Seljuq under-glaze-painted pottery on which undulating leaf-scrolls of very similar form appear [Fig. 26]. Carolinda Tolstoy's `sweeping leaves' have a similar quality of floating energy that go far beyond the natural world from which they ultimately derive. There is a certain magical quality in these patterns, particularly in the pieces that display individual forms freely spaced on the often dark ground, leaving a great deal of undecorated and empty space [Nos. 55 & 57]. Others, although closely relat-

ed to the floating leaf scrolls, retain a closer affinity to natural growing vegetal forms [No. 56]. Still others [No. 63] develop the scroll in a more elaborate and continuous movement; it gives them the quality of the almost infinite self-perpetuation that closely resembles the true Muslim arabesque. These scrolls appear to generate a never-ending perpetuation, other scrolls generating still other scrolls. This much denser scroll pattern is set with small golden leaves that follow the curvilinear movement of the principal scrolls and fill most of the background.

2000 | 19 × 12 cm

2002 | 25 × 14 cm

scrolls | sweeping leaves

2002 | 11 × 29 cm

scrolls | sweeping leaves

2002   25 × 15 cm

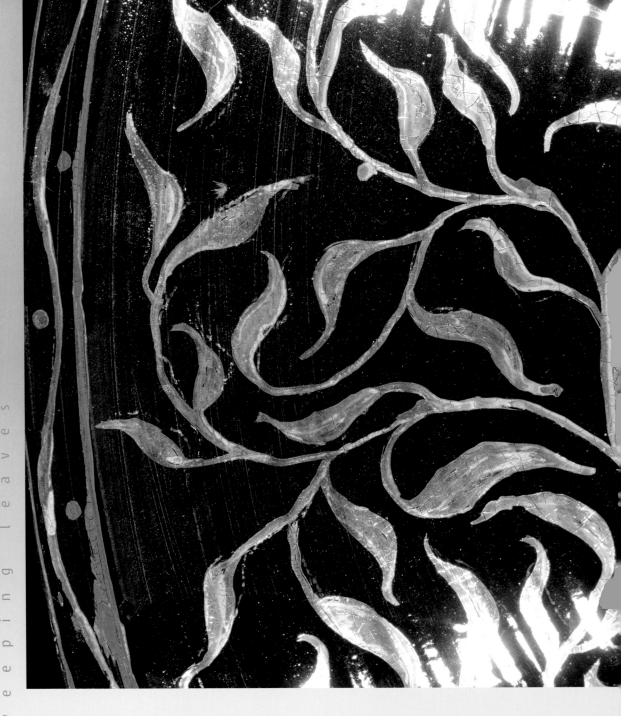

2002 | 29 × 17 cm

c r o l l s | s w e e p i n g   l e a v e s

2002 | 25 × 15 cm

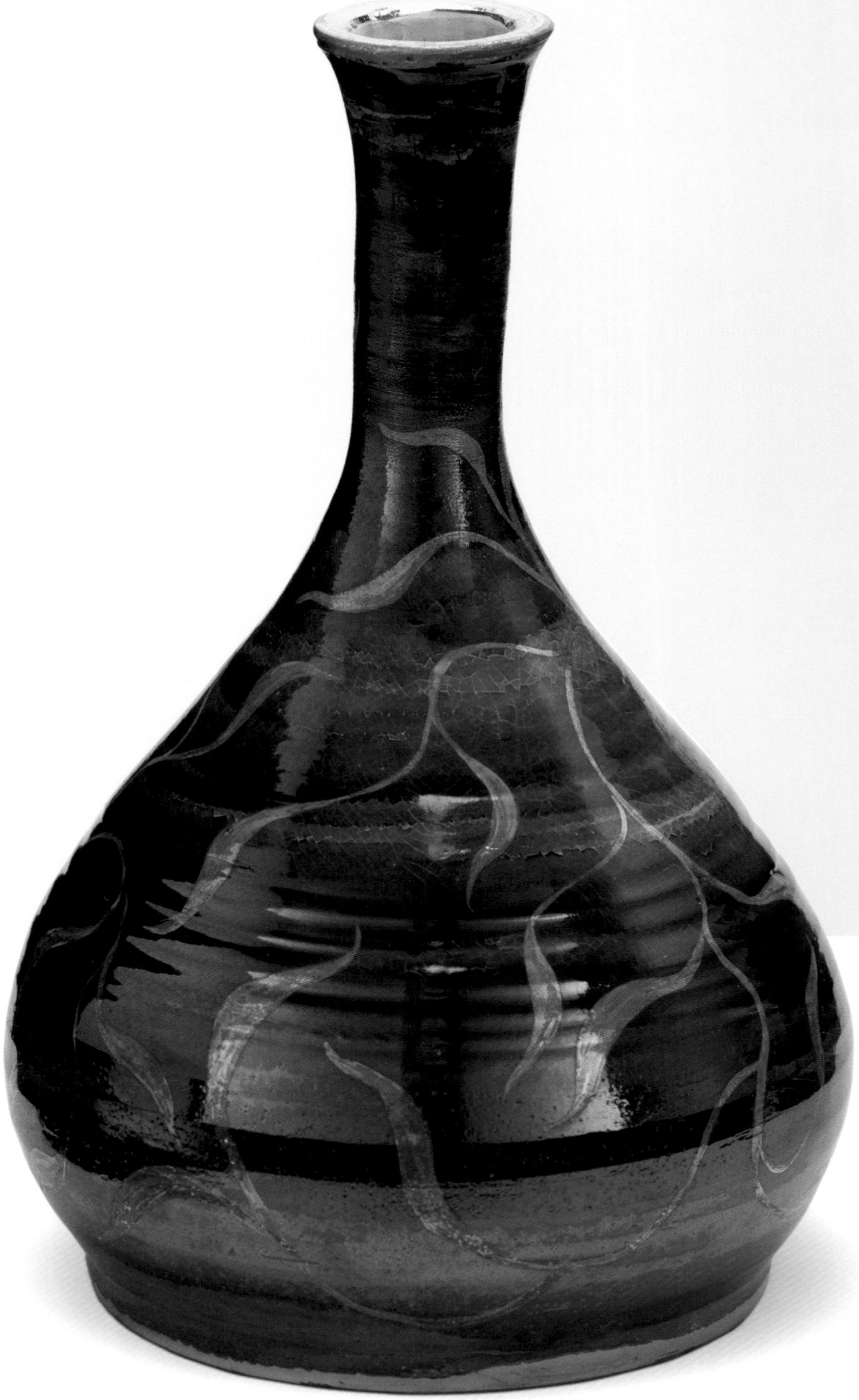

scrolls | sweeping leaves

It is in this group that the scroll patterns achieve a density which covers most of the objects' surfaces: small buds and blossoms, also executed in gold, add to the density of the patterns [Nos. 64 to 68]. A further development, moving towards the fully articulated scroll, takes place in a fourth group.

scrolls | alexandro

scrolls | alexandro

2001 | 39 × 18 cm

2001 | 34 × 17 cm

s c r o l l s | m a n d u

The most elaborate development of the floral scroll appears in a group of objects, labelled [Scrolls 4] by the artist, indicating still a different indebtedness, this time to Indo-Muslim art. Always executed in gold on various deep-coloured backgrounds, the scroll — now terminating in large articulated palmette blossoms — takes on monumental proportions [No. 69]

2003 | 35 × 20 cm

2003 | 36 × 21 cm

scrolls | mandu

2001 10 × 27 cm

A group of objects decorated with floral
shrubs carrying tear-drop shaped blossoms is
closely related, both in their imposing forms
and in their relation to an extraordinarily
wide-spread decorative motif — the so-called
'botteh' — used specifically in 18th and 19th
century India [Nos. 74 to 81]; one thinks especially of the so-called Paisley shawls, all the
rage in 18th and 19th century Europe. From
these designs it is only a small step to the true
quintessential Islamic motif: the Arabesque.

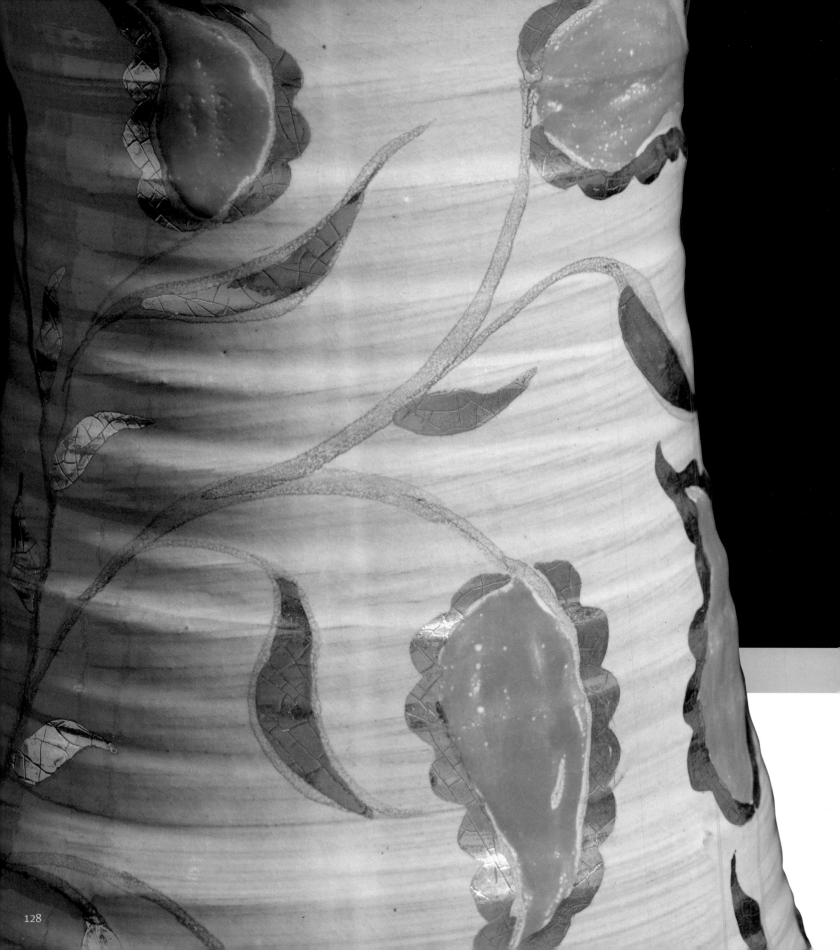

t e a r s

1999 | 13 × 25 cm

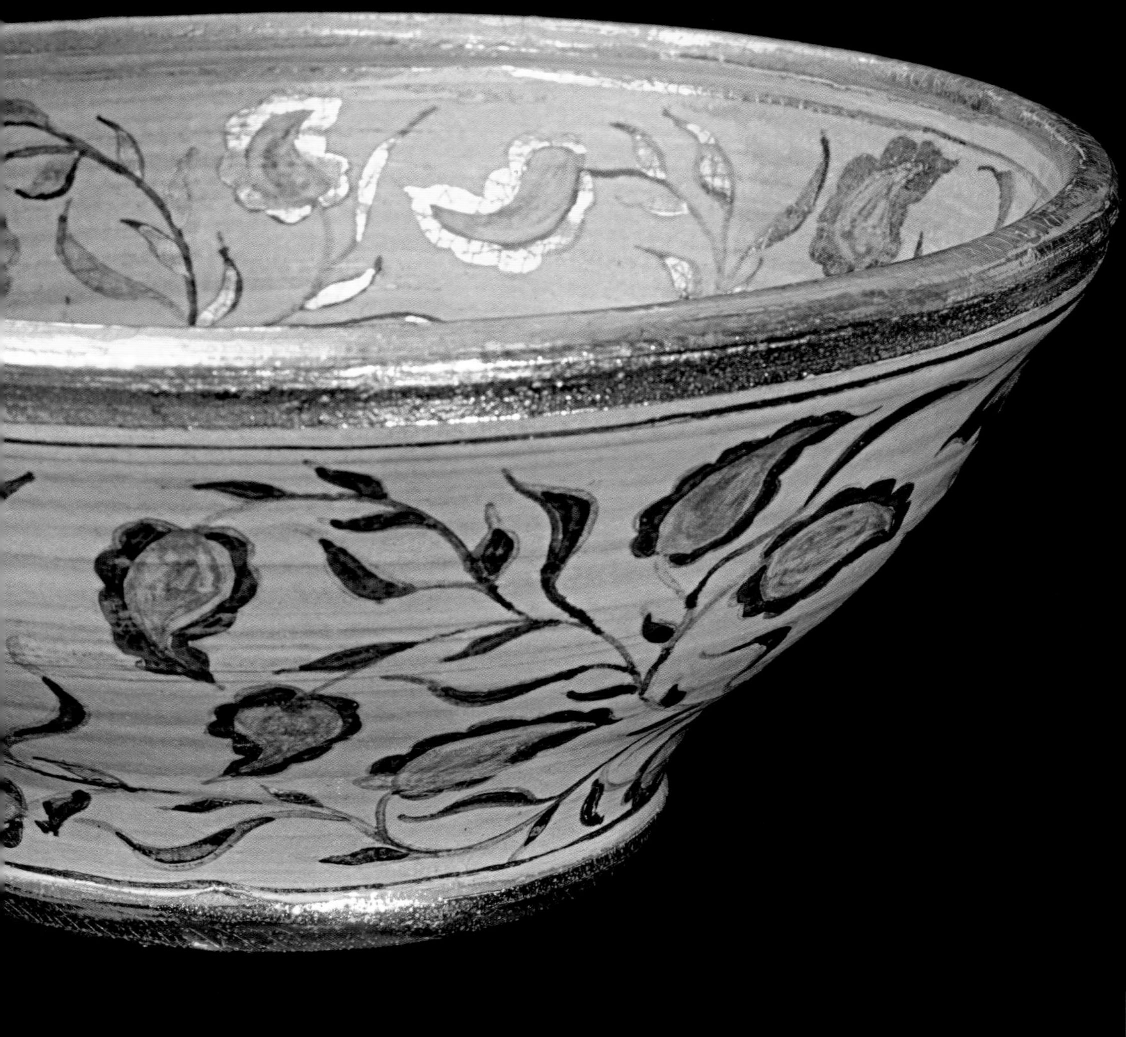

2003 | 26 × 36 cm

Here the small buds or blossoms are developed into larger independent leaf-forms, at times taking the time-honoured shape of the split-palmette [No. 70], an element of Muslim design harking back to pre-Islamic and Classical times that was adopted by Muslim designers in the very first centuries of the Muslim era and has lived on, ever since, into modern times.

Much has been written about the arabesque, but the finest definition is undoubtedly Ernst Kühnel's, who likened the creation of the arabesque to music-making with the drafting pen. He writes (in Richard Ettinghausen's English translation): "It was foremost the artist who carried in himself the Islamic world view to plunge into linear speculations of an abstract nature. He did not create from the memory of what he had seen or experienced but he transferred what we sense to be the natural laws into unreal forms. It was essential that this effort did not degenerate into reckless fantasies but that it led to inspirations which were restrained by deliberate concentration and a disciplined rhythm just as it happens in a musical composition which intentionally submits to thematic and melodic limitations. There must have been an infinite excitement for such music-making with the drafting pen which set out to exhaust within the self-imposed framework all possibilities of a spirited linear configuration." Kühnel, (1976).

Carolinda Tolstoy's designs are perhaps not true arabesques, since they lack the defining quality of the infinitely self perpetuation of the Muslim design — the endless generation of leaves producing leaves from their tips, and blossoms sprouting from the centre of blossoms. Nonetheless, her designs, in their application of a great variety of unrelated, and in this sense 'un-natural' floral forms that are unparalled in the natural world, are closely related to the true arabesque.

2002 | 28 × 15 cm

2003   8 × 37 cm

arabesque

a r a b e s q u e

2000   38 cm 0

a r a b e s q u e

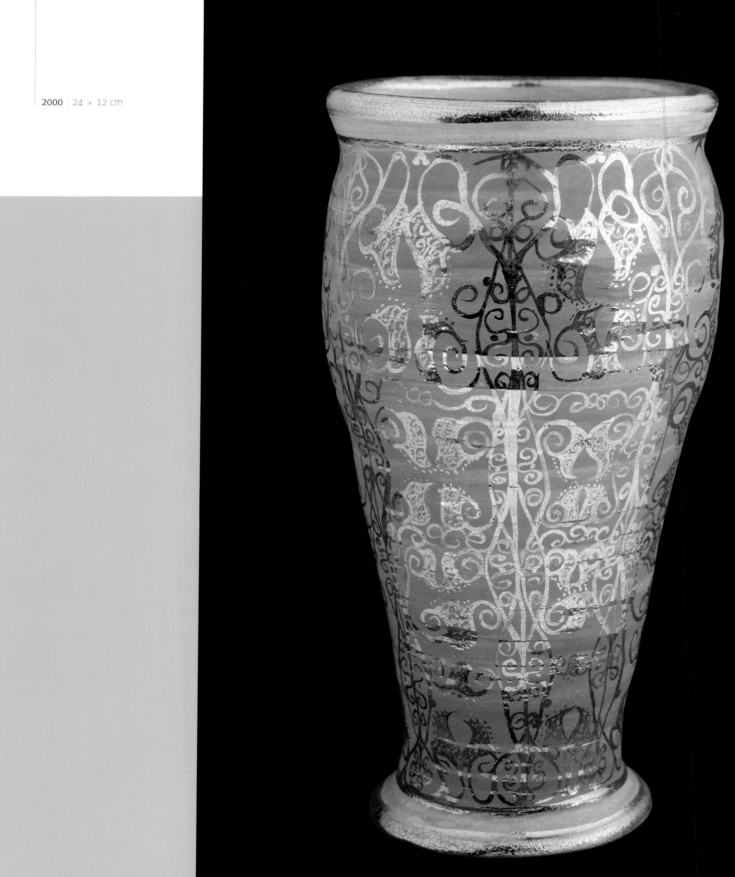

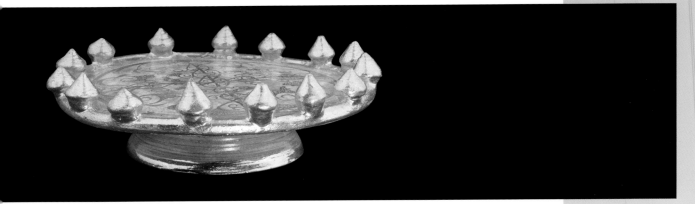

1997 10 × 24 cm

1993 9 × 22 cm

Countess Tolstoy is undoubtedly the major contemporary representative of a considerable English 'Orientalist' tradition. Her work has justly been recognized as perpetuating the fascination of the Western world with Safavid art (see Sheila Canby, *Persian Art* (1999)), while her indebtedness to a truly original interpretation of the Ottoman tradition that can be traced back in an almost uninterrupted line from 16th century Turkey to 17th, 18th and 19th century Italy, France and England, is too obvious to need further insistence or documentation. And it is no surprise to learn that she has recently been commissioned to provide designs for none other than the Deruta factories, which were for such a long time in the forefront of the continuation of these traditions.

You can't Stop the Potter

The making of pots involves two completely different personalities–two such contradictory activities. In fact there are three personalities: Artist, Human Being, and Virtual.

Artist and Human Being: an extreme workaholic with a timetable from 7am to 4am, which starts during the daytime when the Artist needs to work in ceramic art–wetting clay, making vases, firing a kiln, glazing with lustre, firing again, decorating with gold and firing again–and, having a constant hunger to create and to work, continues into the night with firing the kiln. Intertwined within the Artist's life, the Human Being is busy solving the questions of and attending to the needs of three children–Liubov who has just finished studying Russian, Igor embarking on a photographic career and Oleg studying sculpture and design, all three of whom are talented, demanding individuals who need support and encouragement for further development.

There is obviously more than just clay, water, fire and gold in the pots–there is an expression of emotion, feelings and passion: *"I am the pots and the pots are me–one and the same–I don't make the pots, they make themselves through me–they are a natural extension of myself as I am of them–there is only one way the cycle can stop".*

The lustre of the pots is unique, appearing translucent, full of rich colours and different shades of gold. These effects demand extreme skill and experience, a firm hand, perfect control of the temperature of the kiln and the right proportions of gold with the glaze. Yet the Artist does not approach her work in a technical way: *"I evolve with the pots and they with me–we are one and the same–working purely through intuition".*

Or may be it just means that the Artist has reached the level of Master–the state of expressing oneself completely in this very difficult medium–an expression that is extraordinarily sensitive, fragile and very powerful, combined with a determination both to achieve perfection and to convey beauty, sensuality and dreams. In firing her vases and pomegranates, the Artist transforms them from their terracotta, earthy and functional shapes into living and joyful beings.

This book celebrates thirty years of Carolinda's professional life–encompassing studies in Paris and the Chelsea Pottery; travelling and visiting ceramic centres in Manises and Grenada (Spain), Marrakesh and Fez (Morocco), Isfahan, Shiraz and Mashhad (Iran), Herat and Bamiyan (Afghanistan), Istanbul/Constantinople (Turkey), Bukhara, Khiva, Samarkand (Uzbekistan) and the Lomonosov Porcelain Factory, St Petersburg (Russia); and working and teaching in Mytilene (Greece) and the ceramic workshops of Deruta (Italy). In addition, the Artist has already put behind her more than one hundred exhibitions in different venues and parts of the world.

With a passion for reading Persian fairytales on the one hand, Carolinda does not miss attending modern art exhibitions and conceptual performances–she equally can equally be seen at receptions in the embassies of more than half of the world; at the Russian Ballet seasons in the Royal Opera House, Covent Garden; at lectures on Middle Eastern art, including those at the School of Oriental and African Studies and at conceptual and radical modern art performances at Tate Modern.

Moving in these extensive circles of ambassadors, ministers, Russian and Persian aristocrats, Sheikhs, Indian jewellery designers, Middle Eastern ceramic collectors, classical art historians and extreme underground avant-guard artists and composers, evening life is full of events. But the Artist is always to be found with a mini drawing pad hidden in her exquisite Shéhérezade dress which she instantly extracts to catch any new design ideas: *"I am the pot and the decorated clothes are the glaze".*

A recent addiction to collecting contemporary art
has brought into a home already filled with antique
and modern ceramics, new large works by international artists. Yet this eclecticism only serves to enhance
one of the most unusual interiors in London, one which
to her is an environment in which to in work and live.

Then there is also the Virtual Carolinda–a very
strong representation on the Internet. Recognized by
leading global search engines, the Artist comes up
among the top ten results on subjects such as ceramics, golden decoration, Persian dreams, Tolstoy, War &
Peace, pomegranates, Schéhérazade and several other
contradictory, directly related and sometimes unrelated topics. All of which demonstrate the growing popularity of her work and her establishment as a leading
potter, not just among the connoisseurs and collectors
but also among students and the general public.

This is a very special book and event for all of us.

Luke & A

bibliography

Atasoy & Raby, *Iznik* (1989)
Nurhan Atasoy & Julian Raby, *Iznik, The Pottery of Ottoman Turkey*, London, 1989.

Ballardini, "Cantagalli"(1927)
Gaetano Ballardini, "Per la mostra permanente della moderna ceramica italiana d'arte (La manufattura Figli di G. Cantagalli.S.A.J. di Firenze)," *Faenza*, XV, 1927, pp. 69-91, Pls. XVI-XVII.

Caiger-Smith, *Lustre* (1985)
Alan Caiger-Smith, *Lustre Pottery, Technique, tradition and innovation in Islam and the Western World*, London, 1985, Second edition, 1991.

Canby, *Persian Art* (1999)
Sheila Canby, *The Golden Age of Persian Art, 1501-1722*, The British Museum Press, London, 1999. See especially: "Epilogue: The Safavid Legacy," pp. 174-177, where Carolinda Tolstoy's work is shown (p. 177, Fig. 169) as an example of the inspiration which Safavid art provided for twentieth century artists.

Catlin, *De Morgan* (1983)
Jon Catlin, with essays by Elizabeth Aslin and Alan Caiger-Smith, *Willliam De Morgan Tiles*, New York, 1983.

Conti, *Cantagalli* (1982)
Giovanni Conti, *Maioliche Cantagalli in donazione al Bargello/The Bequest of Cantagalli Maiolica to the Bargello*, Florence, 1982 (Lo specchio del Bargello, 9).

Csenky & Steinert, *Zsolnay* (2002)
Eva Csenkey and Agota Steinert (editors), *Hungarian Ceramics from the Zsolnay Manufactory, 1853 — 2001*, Published for The Bard Graduate Center for Studies in the Decorative Arts, Design, and Culture, New York, by Yale University Press, New Haven and London, 2002.

Delft (1984)
Herboren Orient, Islamitisch en Nieuw Delfts Aardwek, Haags Gemeentemuseum, 1984.

Fauvisme (1996)
Keramiek en Fauvisme, Andre Metthey en de schilders, (catalogue of an exhibition) Musée Matisse, Nice, Cimiez, May 17-July 21, 1996, & Stichting Sint-Jan, Brugge, August 3 - November 17, 1996, Brugge & Nice, 1996.

Fontana, "Cantagalli" (1984)
Maria Vittoria Fontana, "L'imitazione europea della ceramica ottomana di Iznik. La fabbrica ottocentesca fiorentina `Figli di G. Cantagalli'," *La Conoscenza dell'Asia e dell'Africa in Italia nei secoli XVII e XIX*, Edited by Ugo Marazzi, Naples, Istituto Universitario Orientale (Collana `Matteo Ripa', III), 1984, I, pp. 727- 747, and Pls. XXXII-XLVII.

Fontana, *Museo Art.Industr.Napoli* (1988)
Maria Vittoria Fontana, *La collezione ceramica islamica e l'imitazione ottocentesca del Museo Artistico Industriale di Napoli, (Taccuni di studi dell'Istituto "F. Palizzi")*, Napoli, 1988.

Gaunt & Clayton-Stamm, *De Morgan* (1971)
William Gaunt and M.D.E. Clayton-Stamm, *William De Morgan*, London, 1971.

Genders, *Inspiration* (2002)
Carolyn Genders, *Sources of Inspiration for ceramics and the applied arts*, London, 2002. Carolinda Tolsatoy's work is being illustrated and discusssed on pp. 28-31.

Gerelyes & Kovacs, *Miklos Zsolnay* (1999)
Ibolya Gerelyes & Orsolya Kovacs, *An unknown Orientalist, The Eastern Ceramics of Miklos Zsolnay*, Pecs- Budapest, 1999.

Haddad, "East & West" (2000)
Rana Haddad, "Somewhere between East & West, The Dreaming Pots of Carolinda Tolstoy," *Craftsman Magazine*, Issue 106, May 2000, pp. 20-22.

Kühnel, *Arabesque* (1976)
Ernst Kühnel, *The Arabesque, Meaning and Transformation of an Ornament*, Translated from the Original Text in German by Richard Ettinghausen, Graz, 1976.

Lane, *Early Isl.Pott.* (1965)
Arthur Lane, *Early Islamic Pottery*, London, 3rd ed.,1965.

Lane, *Later Isl.Pott.* (1957)
Arthur Lane, *Later Islamic Pottery*, London, 1957.

Meath Baker, "Carolinda Tolstoy" (2002)
Elizabeth Meath Baker, "A brush with history, The London ceramist Carolinda Tolstoy," *Cornucopia*, Issue 27, Volume 5, 2002, p. 18.

Vaizey, *Sutton Taylor* (1999)
Marina Vaizey, *Sutton Taylor, A Lustrous Art*, London & Nottingham, 1999.

Wedgwood, *Wedgwood Coll.* (1993)
Barbara Wedgwood, *Three Centuries of Wedgwood, The Ceramic Collection of Barbara & Hensleigh Wedgwood*, Dallas, 1993.

Wilson, *Ital.Ren* (1987)
Timothy Wilson, *Ceramic Art of the Italian Renaissance*, London, 1987

notes on the illustrations

Fig. 1 Plate with floral pattern and gilded decoration
Turkey, Iznik, 16th century
New York, The Metropolitan Museum of Art,
acc.no. 52.1.19

Fig. 2 Plate with floral pattern in the Ottoman style
Candia (Padua), dated 1661
Private Collection, Italy

Fig. 3 Plate with floral pattern in the Ottoman style
Florence, Cantagalli factory, mid-19th century
London, Private Collection

Fig. 4 Plate with Ottoman style floral pattern,
Hungary, Zsolnay factory, Pecs, 1879
(see Gerelyes & Kovacs, *Miklos Zsonay*
[1999], Fig. 46).
Pecs, Janus Pannonius Museum,
inv.no. JPM 51.1482.1

Fig. 5 Twin handled amphora with Ottoman floral pattern
designed by William De Morgan, Fulham period,
1888-1897
(see Gaunt & Clayton-Stamm, *De Morgan* [1971],
Fig. 128).

Fig. 6 Tiles designed by William de Morgan
(see Gaunt & Clayton-Stamm, *De Morgan* [1971],
Fig. 19).

Fig. 7 Bowl with lutre-painted decoration
designed by William De Morgan, late Fulham period
Clayton Stamm Collection
(see Gaunt & Clayton-Stamm, *De Morgan* [1971],
Fig. 111).

Fig. 8 Jar with winged handles
(Alhambra-Vase type)

Spain, Manises, after 1465,
made for the Medici family,
London, The British Museum, Godman Bequest,
1983, G 619
(see Wilson, *Ital.Ren*. [1957], col.pl. 16).

Fig. 9 Two-handled maiolica vase, Italy, Deruta,
about 1515
London, The Victoria and Albert Museum
(see Caiger-Smith, *Lustre* [1985], col.pl. XV).

Fig. 10 Plate with red-lustre decoration
Italy, Gubbio, about 1525-1530
New York, The Robert Lehman Collection, The
Metropolitan Museum
of Art, acc.no. 1975.1.1108

Fig. 11 Bowl with lustre-painted dcoration
England, Wedgwood factory, 1934
London, Private Collection

Fig. 12 Lustre painted vase, Plikington factory,
about 1880.
London, Private Collection.

Fig. 13 Four lustre-painted tiles
designed by William De Morgan,
Fulham period, 1888-1897
London, The Victoria and Albert Museum,
inv.no. E 558-1917

Fig. 14 Lustre-painted tile
London, Maw factory, about 1880
London, Private Collection

Fig. 15 Alan Caiger-Smith,
Lustre-painted bowl, 1982

Fig. 16 Polychrome lustre-painted bowl
Iraq, Abbasid period, 9th century
Ham, Keir Collection

Fig. 17 Sutton Taylor, Lustre painted bowl, 1980

(see Vaizey, *Sutton Taylor* [1999], Pl. 2).

Fig. 18 Sutton Taylor, Lustre-painted bowl, 1986
(see Vezay, *Sutton Taylor* [1999], Pl. 5).

Fig. 19 Variegated lustre vase, Wedgwood, ca. 1810
(see *The Barbara & Heinsleigh Wedgwood Collection*
[1993], Fig. 75).

Fig. 20 Bowl with lustre-painted decoration in the
Seljuq style
The Netherlands, Delft, about 1910
The Hague, Gemeentemuseum, inv.no. MC 14-1984
(see *Delft* [1984], p. 45).

Fig. 21 Lion-handled bowl with lustre-painted decoration in the Seljuq style
The Netherlands, Delft, about 1930
The Hague, Gemeentemuseum, inv.no. MC 13-1984

Fig. 22 Plate with Ottoman style floral decoration
The Netherlands, Delft, about 1910
The Hague, Gemeentemuseum, inv.no. MC 1-1984

Fig. 23 André Metthey, Ceramic star tile
Paris, Private Collection
(see *Fauvisme* [1996], p. 57).

Fig. 24 André Matthey, Ceramic dish
Paris, Musee de Petit Palais
(See *Fauvisme* [1996], p. 74).

Fig. 25 Henri Matisse, Ceramic vase, 1907
Nice, Musée Matisse
(see *Fauvisme* [1996], p. 85).

Fig. 26 Maurice de Vlamick, Ceramic plate
about 1907-1909
Paris, Musée de l'art moderne.
(see *Fauvisme* [1996], p. 115).

Fig. 27 Underglaze-painted ceramic bowl
Persia, 12th -13th century

exhibitions and work history

permanent exhibitions

2003	Primavera, Cambridge
2002	Garden of Eden Gallery, London
2002	SUAV Gallery, KUSAV Foundation, Turkish Culture, Istanbul, Turkey
2002	Dar al Funoon, Kuwait
2002	The Watts Gallery, Compton
2002	AYA Gallery, London
2001	School of Oriental & African Studies, London
2001	Saray Gallery, London

selected exhibitions

solo exhibitions

2003	Barbican Centre, London
2003	Ancient Mesopotamia to Modern Iraq – Royal Geographical Society, London
2002	Iran and the World in the Safavid Age – Brunei Gallery, London
2002	Hali Fair, Olympia Exhibition Centre, London
2001/1999	School of Oriental & African Studies, London University
2001	Centre Culturel Arabe Syrien, Paris
1993/92/91	Ergami Studio, Mytilene, Greece
1983	The Maltings, Farnham

joint exhibitions

2003/2002	Garden of Eden Gallery, London
2002	Dar al Funoon, Kuwait
2001	'Greece in Britain 2001', Hellenic Centre, London
1999	Piers Feetham Gallery, London

group exhibitions

2003/02/01	Garden of Eden Gallery, London
2002	SUAV Gallery, KUSAV Foundation, Turkish Culture, London
2002	Dar al Fanoon, Kuwait
2001/99	The Gallery in Cork Street, London
2001	Collins & Hastie Ltd, London
2001/00	The Garden Door Gallery, London
2000	The Royal College of Art, London
1997	Gallery K, London
1976	The Brotherton Gallery, London

potteries

1978	Carolinda Tolstoy Pottery, London
1973 – 1980	The Chelsea Pottery, London

apprenticeship

1973 – 1980	The Chelsea Pottery, London

guest designer

2003	Umbaldo Grazia Maioliche Artstiche Artigianali, Detrua, Italy
2003	Umbaldo Grazia Maioliche Artstiche Artigianali, Detrua, Italy
1993 – 1996	Dadi Ceramique, Paris
1990 – 1993	Ergami Ceramic Studio, Mytilene, Grecce

teaching

1976 – 1980	The Chelsea Pottery, London

masterclasses

2003	Royal College of Art, London
2003	Camberwell School of Art, London
2003	Victoria and Albert Museum, London
2001	Central St Martin's School of Art, London
2001	The Iran Society, London
2000	School of Oriental & African Studies, London University
1999	Ceradel, Paris
1998	Camberwell School of Art, London
1990 – 1993	Ergami Ceramic Studio, Mytilene, Greece

broadcasting

2002	Independent Republic of Iran Broadcasting – Jaam-e-Jam
2001	BBC World Service
2001	Independent Republic Iran Broadcasting – Jaam-e-Jam
1999	Iranian Broadcasting Co

Stockists

2003	Ubaldo Grazia Maioliche Artstiche Artigianali, Detrua, Italy
2002	Renwick & Clarke, London
1977 – 1987	General Trading Company Ltd., London

Istanbul Heritage Fund

Luke & A Gallery
London • Vienna

First published by Art Books International 2003
Unit 007, The Chandlery, 50 Westminster Bridge Road, SE1 7QY

ISBN 1 874044 56 2

Consultancy and supervision Luke & A. Gallery

Designed by Anikst Design
Misha Anikst and Alfonso Iacurci

Photography:
Front Cover by Igor Tolstoy
Rodney Todd White & Son, Igor Tolstoy, Joss Reiver Bany and fA

Edited by Eleanor Sims, Janet Rady, Liubov Tolstoy and Paulina Ivanova

ernst j.grube

a brief biography

Born in Austria, May 9, 1932; educated in Berlin, Germany

1955	Ph.D., Freie Universitat, Berlin
1955-1958	Assistant to Ernst Kuhnel, Berlin Museum
1958	Joined The Metropolitan Museum of Art, New York
1962-1968	Curator of Islamic Art at The Metropolitan Museum of Art; at the same time Adjunct Professor of Islamic Art at Columbia University in New York
1968-1972	Professor of Medieval, Islamic and Far Eastern Art at the City University of New York (HunterCollege)
1972	Appointed Professor of Islamic Art at the University of Padua, Italy
1973	Began, also, to teach Islamic Art at the Oriental Institute in Naples, Italy
1972-1978	Member of the Italian Archaeological Mission in Iran
1977-1988	Professor of Islamic Art at the University of Venice, Italy
1980	Established the annual Islamic Art, Editor with Eleanor Sims, now published jointly by the East - West Foundation, New York, and The Bruschettini Foundation of Islamic and Asian Art, Genoa
1988	Retired from the University of Venice; since then, mainly engaged in research and writing on Islamic art

acknowledgments

Dedicated to my parents and my children Liubov, Igor and Oleg

Working in harmony for over thirty years William George Bell and Fiona Dadi

Introduction to ceramics
Martis Culucundis and Andrei Tolstoy
constant advice and support over the years Sam Ala, Joan Bowles, Nadine Bonsor, Sheila Canby, Moya Carey, Robert Döry, Annabel Fairfax, Alexandra Gibbs, Shusha Guppy, Maria Halkiadis, Brian Hubbard, Tania Illingworth, Nadine Killearn, Sara Keuhns, Joyce Morgan, Nigel Newbury, Zelfa Olivier, Huw Owen-Jones, Ruth du Pré, Janet Rady, Soussi Kerman Rastegar, Nancy Stewart, Naomi Wölffer

Multi inspirational
Alexander Barabanov, Robert Bucknall, Mitchel Abdul Karim Crites, Leonidas Vostanis

Exhibitions, photography and computer
Dobrinka Jevtich, Dushan Jevtich, Artis Lismanis, Igor Tolstoy, Oleg Tolstoy, fraAlexandro & saintLuka (Luke & A. Gallery of Modern Art)

Gulya Diarova (Garden of Eden Gallery) for her dedication to continually exhibiting my work

Including all those whom I may have forgotten to mention.